SHAZAM!
THE FORMULA
for Getting What You Really, Really, Really Want! When All Seems Lost, It Ain't!

Dr. Scout Cloud Lee

BALBOA.
PRESS
A DIVISION OF HAY HOUSE

Scripture quotations are taken from The Living Bible copyright
© 1971. Used by permission of Tyndale House Publishers, Inc.,
Carol Stream, Illinois 60188. All rights reserved.

Balboa Press books may be ordered through booksellers or by contacting:

Balboa Press
A Division of Hay House
1663 Liberty Drive
Bloomington, IN 47403
www.balboapress.com
1 (877) 407-4847

Because of the dynamic nature of the Internet, any web addresses or links contained in
this book may have changed since publication and may no longer be valid. The views
expressed in this work are solely those of the author and do not necessarily reflect the
views of the publisher, and the publisher hereby disclaims any responsibility for them.

The author of this book does not dispense medical advice or prescribe the use of any
technique as a form of treatment for physical, emotional, or medical problems without the
advice of a physician, either directly or indirectly. The intent of the author is only to offer
information of a general nature to help you in your quest for emotional and spiritual well-
being. In the event you use any of the information in this book for yourself, which is your
constitutional right, the author and the publisher assume no responsibility for your actions.

Print information available on the last page.

ISBN: 978-1-9822-2716-6 (sc)
ISBN: 978-1-9822-2717-3 (e)

Balboa Press rev. date: 10/17/2019

CONTENTS

THE FORMULA

$$ABCDE+L3+W2(+/-X) = PMA$$

The "Secret" is out. Now
THE FORMULA brings together all the pieces
of The Secret and beyond into a step-by-step way
to co-create what you really, really, really want in
your beautiful life! When all seems lost, it ain't!

DEDICATION

Contributions to this work are dedicated to this sweet Mother Earth, and the Great Spirit of Life and Love that flows through all things. We have walked with Spirit and lived into these truths. We are grateful to have never walked alone. May this work find its way into the hands of kings and queens and teens and everyone in between. May those who seek profound healing and glorious prosperity find within, the power that is Peace, and pass it on.

Dr. Scout Cloud Lee

THE **FORMULA** FOR GETTING WHAT YOU REALLY, **REALLY, REALLY** WANT!

By: Dr. Scout Cloud Lee

"May the Force be with you" is charming but not important. What's important is that you become the Force". Harrison Ford

January 7th, 1990, will forever be one of the most important turning points in my life. It was a cold winter night in Oklahoma. We built a big fire in our fireplace and stretched out on the couch to enjoy some mindless television. You could have knocked me over with a feather when I reached up to scratch under my right arm, and discovered a large "growth" the size of a golf ball. It must have come up suddenly and it didn't hurt. This, I took as good news until I called my surgeon friend, who informed me that it was probably cancer. The fact that it didn't hurt was not a good sign.

This was a time of my life when I did not have medical insurance. The possibility of cancer was not good news. I decided to change my diet by adding lots of "orange and green" stuff, and I accepted a consulting job in Florida where I could focus on running and a healthier lifestyle. I have since come to believe that there are five things necessary for a happy, healthy life. We must **hydrate** (preferably with water), **sweat**, **laugh**, **unite with others** and **poop** daily. I'm not one to preach a particular diet or exercise as "the way, the truth and the light". I just believe that by doing these five things, however we choose to do them, will give us a good shot at being happy and healthy. At first, these five things may seem overly simple. However, it takes depth and discipline to live a lifestyle that allows for each of these daily habits.

My time in Florida proved beneficial. I stashed some extra money, lost some weight, and focused on my health. The "growth" seemed to shrink a little. Four months into my Florida work, I dreamed a powerful dream. I had walked into an office and been greeted by a red-headed doctor in a white lab coat. The next afternoon I was returning from our country-based training site when I caught a glimpse of a sign out of the corner of my eye. It read, "Family Surgery. Walk-ins Welcome". I had passed the building before and thought it was a veterinary clinic. I turned around and parked. It was almost closing time. When I walked into the clinic I was met by a red-headed doctor in a white lab coat. Fifteen minutes later I was scheduled for "next day surgery" with the prognosis that I probably had cancer. I notified my family in Oklahoma.

The following morning I awakened early to the sight of a fading sign from dream time. It read, "The angels walk with you". Eight hours later I was sitting in my hospital room with three friends and my doctor. "Get your life in order! You have approximately two months to live". At age 45 I received the "wake up call" of my life. **What I chose to do next has made all the difference in the world.** Everything that I had ever believed or taught was called into question. It was truly time to "put up or shut up".

I couldn't help but weep for my possible loss and my family's loss. My tears were short lived. News traveled fast and I began to receive all manner of cards, books, and recommended diets, all of which reinforced the possibility of the "truth of the prognosis"; "Two months to live". The gifts of my friends and family all spelled "Cancer" in big, bold letters. Gratefully, these gifts sent me into a day long, deep meditation and contemplation. I checked deep inside to find my own reality. I discovered two important things. First of all, I re-affirmed my deep and abiding relationship with that which I call God. I decided if God wanted me to come home, I was ready. Secondly, I decided to focus on my **life over my death**. The grass needed mowing, so I mowed. I had songs in me that had not been written and recorded, so I moved to Nashville and began recording my music. (I've since recorded four CD's). While in Nashville, the grass needed mowing, so I mowed. I discovered a book in me that needed to be written, so I wrote. I continued to live.

I returned home to Oklahoma to fix fences and start training my young colts. I continued to live. I wrote more songs and more books. The grass needed mowing, so I mowed. To this very day, the grass still needs mowing, so I mow. For as long as God gives me breath, I will "mow over die".

It has been said that there is but one great success: To live your life according to your heart's desire. And, living life according to your heart's desire takes enormous courage. It takes the courage to live life in your own way, come hell, high water, or worst of all, normality. What passes for sanity in this world scares the holy, living bejesus out of me. We all long to be souls unshackled, spirits walking free. Yet, we're still in bodies that require constant love and care. At no time is that more evident than when a physician looks us in the face and declares, "You have cancer!" I have since discovered that the possibility of losing my ranch or worse, losing the most precious love of my life to an affair, is another form of "wake up" call. As long as we live and draw breath, we are called to "practice what we preach" and clarify what we truly believe is possible.

Most people spend much of life playing hide and seek with themselves. We don't have a clue who we are or what we want until some earth shattering news wakes us up. At times like these some people play "hide and quit". This book is about how to play **Hide and Be Found**! It's about fighting and winning the right to protect our divine, unique destiny and our own special dreams. It's about saying a big "Adios, Toodle lew, Roger Wilco, I'm out of here, Good-bye and Ā hui hou to *shoulda', coulda', woulda', and "yessuh, Boss, what eva' you says"*. It's a book about living life full-out in the face of devastating odds. It's a book with a simple and powerful **FORMULA for playing the co-creation game with God**, The Universe, The Great All-That-Is, The Great Doo Da, Ga Ga, and every other name for the Great Provider Gaming Spirit That Dwells Within. It's a book about surviving and thriving through cancer, marital affairs, bankruptcy and other bad stuff. It's a book about Holy and Divine Magic. It's a book about our Sacred technology that allows us to be accountable for our well-being, as well as all the crap we attract. When all seems lost, this is a very good book to read, absorb, and live full-out. WHEN ALL SEEMS LOST, IT'S TIME FOR HOLY AND DIVINE MAGIC!

I'm writing this book because it's a book I want to read. I'm not striving to be holy, sacred, or "blessed among women". I'm not even trying to be a good Girl Scout! This book was simply noise in my head that needed to be silenced by nailing these words to a page and sending them out to you. We are each a knowing in touch with all knowing". We are each a" mystery living inside the Great Mystery". We are "forever spirits" having a very temporary human experience. If we're not enjoying our lives, we're not fulfilling our divine purpose. Period! If we are faced with devastating odds, we must learn to trust principles that we have read about or tried to live.

We all, at times, try to chink every little crack in our soul with ritual, and ceremony, and reading books just like this one. But reading this book won't vault anyone out of despair, save a life, or push someone up the corporate ladder. That is, it won't do a darn thing unless these principles in THE FORMULA are practiced and found to be useful. There is nothing new under the sun. We've just gathered up the pieces of thinkers before and put it all into a simple formula that, at the very most may save your life, and at the very least will cost you the dedication of life, limb, and devotion. The payback is the discovery of yourself, your passage beyond devastation, and your own Divine Technology for creation that will bring you your own personal "Big Happy" in business and life.

I was forced to discover and live these principles when I was diagnosed with cancer. My very life depended on it. I often sought the silence and listened to my own heart. I was touched with life-shaking visions, and ended up with a career different than I imagined. Since the day of my cancer diagnosis, I've made the journey to hell and back several times, and tested and retested this material. I'm now writing about life, living beyond cancer, healing, and manifesting the reality I want in my life. I do so as I best understand and experience it. This vision and this material could not be bought for a fee to a workshop. I've paid for this vision with my life. The story of this book chose me. I want to pass it on in the hopes that someone will take a chance on themselves and end up with their best life and the Greatest Love of All.

Bottom line, I love simplicity! In fact, I've convinced myself that simplicity is true genius. Our mentors raised us with this advice, "Live and Let Live", "Give when you're asked" and "It ain't none of my business". Sounds pretty simple. Yet it has taken over 50 years of research, lots of life experience, living through a "two months to live cancer prognosis", losing my mate, and becoming both an unsuccessful and successful professional in order to synthesize these powerful teachings into "The Formula". THE FORMULA consistently works. "THE FORMULA" gives us a set of tools that immediately supports living life with ease, joy, passion, and insatiable humor. THE FORMULA is a creative dance with God. THE FORMULA is an investment in surviving and THRIVING in business and in life.

Einstein is best remembered for a simple formula: E = MC2. Energy equals any mass times it's constant, squared. Units of measurement are facts. Math is a constant that has spawned the compelling television show "Numbers" in which crimes are solved with numbers and formulas.

In 2001 Russell Crowe brilliantly portrayed John Forbes Nash Jr. in the award winning movie A BEAUTIFUL MIND. This math prodigy was able to solve problems that baffled the greatest minds. Forbes was a brilliant, asocial mathematician who made an astonishing discovery early in his career. After a long journey into hell, he emerged triumphant over his personal tragedy. Late in his life he received the Nobel Prize for his formula for "Togetherness", or the power of group alignment.

Sometimes, in order to save your own life, you have to get freaking "REAL".The Formula came one day on a walk with friends. We experienced a major "AHA!!!". A BIG OMG (Oh My GOD!). It was so simple, and yet so profound that it rocked us to our core. Together we rejoiced, "Free! Free at last!" On this day "The Formula" found us and I devoted my life to living it full out. "The Formula", quite literally, saved my life! Here it is. The rest of this book details each aspect of The Formula.

THE FORMULA: ABCDE + L3+W2 (+/- X) = PMA

A= *Ask (Be specific)*

B = *Believe (That it is already a reality that you are living)*

C = *Celebrate (In advance of the thing/experience "showing up")*

D = *Delegate (Trust enough to put it in God's pocket and leave it there)*

E = *Easy does it.* (*Relax knowing that you have done your most important part*)

L3 = *Live* it, as though you have that thing/experience. Count your blessings.
Let Live. Let others live their lives. You live yours.
Let Grow. Now leave it alone and let it grow and blossom. Trust!

W2 = *Win/Win* (*Seek always to have everyone get the most of what they want. Everyone wins!*)
X = *Personal Choice or Preference* in all things great and small (*Now CHOOSE to move toward or away from all things that equal health, professional prosperity, love. friends, home, personal habits, etc.*)
PMA = *Positive Mental Attitude* (*at the very least*) or (*at the very most*) *POWERFUL MANIFESTATION ACTIVATED*

Positive Mental Attitude and POWERFUL MANIFESTATION ACTIVATED is firmly established as the Attractive Force in the universe. However, "PMA is hard work", states a leather-skinned old hippy from the North shore of Kauai. "Every day I wake up with a cup of coffee and some good ole' PMA. The PMA is hard".

We've long since learned that positive mental attitude is challenged every day, every hour, every minute. It takes intention and focus to maintain PMA throughout the day! The Formula makes the challenge exciting and profoundly simple. Of course, the first challenge is to know WHAT YOU WANT! Belief and FAITH in the power of the Universe to deliver is huge! And, most people wait for the thing/ experience to come before they celebrate. Most often "the thing" never comes. It works just the opposite. We must celebrate in advance of "it" coming.

"Live It and Let Live" allows us to do just that. Mind our own business! Give when asked. Go where we are welcomed. Respect peoples' chosen paths. Take care of your own "stuff" rather than attempting to "fix/help/rescue" others. Focus on increasing and maintaining inner peace. It really is a full time job. Everyone has lessons to learn, and we must let them learn in their own way. We have all experienced bottomless foolishness. How wisdom finds us is a personal thing. "Letting Grow" is a discipline. It's so tempting to continue to revisit our requests, but seeds can't grow if we keep plucking them up to take a peek.

The greatest gift of our humanity is our freedom of CHOICE. The Great Doo Da Ga Ga by all names, created us in our totally Divine Image of Love, and then "cut us FREE". Always, the choice is ours. We simply move from one choice to the next. We are constantly living into our "preferences". When we "Live It and Let Live", we have no need for judgments. We are all free to choose! We simply need to make choices when another's "living" impacts our own "living". Then we must consider W2 (Win/Win). PMA results when we do so with a Win/Win attitude. "Right and Wrong" need not exist. Simply "win/win". Where any two situations clash, there is common ground. Working from "common ground", we simply move into a result that all can value.

Both L3 and W2 need the freedom to expand or contract. We can choose to "X" or "Add" anything, to include people, places, things, thoughts, feelings, and experiences. The act of adding or subtracting is always an act of "preference". We need not make a final, lifetime decision. We only need to prefer a thought, feeling or experience, and move into it. The result of "getting real" with our preferences moves us to Positive Mental Attitude and Powerful Manifestation Activated. THE FORMULA may well hold the key to the transforming power of simplicity, wellness, and personal happiness. It is easy to memorize and utilize, and includes the fun of noticing "violations". We often tease each other with "Opps! Violation of L3! Live,

Let Live, Let Grow!" May THE FORMULA bring love, laughter, health and gratitude to your path. May it help you in "becoming the Force".

Have faith! Faith is when you cannot see HOW, but you absolutely know that THE MOMENT YOU HAVE THE DREAM it is given to you, and all you have to do is RELAX and ALLOW the Universe to magnetize YOU TO YOUR DREAM and YOUR DREAM TO YOU.

Have faith! Have Fun! Be well and Prosper!

Scout Cloud Lee

Chapter One

ASK!

ABCDE+L3+W2 (+/-X) = PMA

"And so it is – keep on asking and you will keep on getting; keep on looking and you will keep on finding, knock and the door will be opened. Everyone who asks, receives; all who seek, find: and the door is opened to everyone who knocks". Luke 11:9-10 – THE BOOK

Thinking and saying exactly what you really want takes enormous energy. Asking for it takes guts, balls, self-love, and bone chilling honesty. Few people know what they really want. Hell, they can't even think of a freaking something to wish for when they toss a penny in the well! In fact, it's scarier than jack crap to realize that most people are scattered from breakfast

1

to hell and back to supper again! Spouting off "what we don't want" is easier than slappin' mosquitoes in a swamp. But when we ask, like a broken record, "Well, WHAT <u>DO</u> YOU WANT?" we're met with the look of a catatonic faced with the challenge of delivering the Gettysburg Address! Circle, ball, chain, 'round and 'round we go searching for the words to wrap around the desires of our heart. We hem and haw, stew and fret, and almost never do the simple thing. *ASK!* Mostly, we just don't think of it.

Too often we feel unworthy to ask for something just because we want it. Asking for what we want is a formidable task. It requires collecting ourselves into one place, with clear vision into our own inner space. It takes the vocabulary of a child sitting on Santa's lap spouting a Christmas wish list. It takes loving ourselves enough to believe that we are worthy. It takes making a picture so utterly amazing that we can say, "There has never been a better time than this to step into this picture!" We must make a picture so beautiful that it almost makes us salivate to look at it! In my case, no matter what, the picture must read, "Animals Welcome, Of Course!"

There is nothing that we ask for that doesn't set the Universe in motion immediately. Nothing! Even pause and hesitation whistles up pause and hesitation.

Our words of asking are like arrows aimed directly at God! We must see a distant target and feel certain of our aim. We must weed all doubt from our mind, point our words like arrows directly at our target, take a deep breath, hold it, and loose the arrow of our words directly into God's safe keeping. I simply "put it in God's pocket".

Puka Romo was fourteen years old and the youngest member of a gathering in the woods outside Toronto. Each person simply had the task of speaking their name and stating their purpose in joining the group. Fifty adults mumbled, hemmed, hawed and "huhed" their way through the introductions. Then came Puka. He took a giant step forward into the circle, squared up his shoulders and announced his name: ***"My name is Puka Romo and I'm here to share fun, laughter, and love!"*** You could have blown the entire circle of adults over with a feather. Don't you know the Grand All-That-Is summoned legions of angels to surround Puka that instant and bring about his wish! Now let's see, "Shall we invest in Bob who just slinked away from his own name, or Puka who owns himself in his totality?" Duhhhhh! It is not just the words spoken, but the power of the words and the ***tone*** of delivery that makes the difference. Our thoughts, words, feelings, and expression of those feelings unfailingly become the things and events of our lives. Unfailingly!

Sometimes life is as clear as The Hallelujah Chorus thundering in our ears. At other times we can't see beyond the end of our noses. Always we are riding a dream. It's just that the dream is so often not our own. In times like these we need to take special care. What we think about we bring about. We need to stop and get clear. We need to take care *before* asking so that we need never feel regret. If we put "it" out right, it'll come back right. If we put "it" out confused and conflicted, "it'll" come back confused and conflicted. When we put out "kind'a like, and sort'a and maybe like" it all comes back to us "kind'a like, sort'a and maybe". We spend the next fifteen years tryin' to get out of all the "sort'a likes" we blindly breathed into the Universe.

"Intent is everything". An *"intent"* set is a seed planted that will bare harvest in-spite-of our distractions and detours. The sages of All Time know this thing: *Intend well. Project intention into that place that serves Divine Will and always ask that All be served in the highest possible way.* To ask clearly is to firmly set an intention into the clay of the Universe. It is the first step in Holy and Divine Magic.

1989 was marked by a steaming hot summer and a cold, snowy winter in Oklahoma. The mice were unusually busy on the Ranch. We decided to get a "barn cat" to help out with the mice. That seems like an ordinary idea to anyone living in the country. However, for us, the idea of making a cat sleep in the barn defies our reputation for "totally spoiling" all our animals. However, we bucked up and firmly planted our intention upon getting a "barn cat".

The want ads listed two locations for "free kittens". We arranged to see both litters. Our first stop brought us into direct contact with three of the cutest little black kittens on earth. We couldn't decide, so took all three. The afternoon stop again connected us with three of the cutest little red kittens on earth. Again, we couldn't decide and took all three. We arrived back at The Ranch with six little kittens ready to take up residence in the barn.

Our plan seemed immediately foiled when we realized that these little ones would have to endure the bitter winter in the barn. It was with some degree of guilt that we prepared their winter bed, put out food and water and played with them for hours. We were awakened early the next morning with yowling like none other. We raced to the barn to discover dead kittens scattered everywhere. One little red kitten came screaming across the yard dragging his back leg. We were horrified. Our young American bull dog had found those "strangers" in the barn and proceeded to take them out. She got to wear a dead kitten wired to her collier for three days, just long enough to learn never to repeat such an act. Over her 14 years she never even dared look at a cat.

By now we were sorely aware that our "intent" was way off base. First of all, the kittens would take a year or more to develop an interest in mice. Secondly, our "excess" of six versus one came back to us. Little red quickly got named "Lion" and nestled inside the ranch house to be nurtured and healed. He stayed there all winter.

In late Spring we neutered Lion, who was now quite spoiled. It would be impossible to describe the look on his face over the whole process. He simply couldn't believe that such a regal being as he would be forced to endure such a process. He took off for a couple of days to protest. Then three, then five, then a week, then two. Soon Lion was gone only to be sighted every month or so. He would show himself from a distance and let us know that he was still around, but took on all the traits of a truly wild Lion. This went on for seven years.

Then the severe winter winds blew in and Lion begin to come closer. He began to yowl and invite connection. We put food out for him and gradually moved it closer to the barn. It took a full two weeks to coax him into the barn to eat and live. It took another four months to actually touch him.

Each day I began my day by feeding our horses, llamas, and donkeys. Then I carried fresh water and food to Lion in the barn where I climbed up on the hay to his nest. There we cuddled and purred and prayed together. Over eight years passed between the time we set an *INTENT* to have a barn cat to help with the mice and the actual realization of that intent. Not a day went by without Lion and I setting *"intentions"* together, because he was my strongest teacher of this profound spiritual truth. Intend well! ASK CLEARLY! We must ask clearly and know that we are worthy of receiving.

The very first sin at which we become accomplished is lying to ourselves. In truth, we are profoundly worthy, and beautiful and powerful and blameless. But we suck up other's assessments of us until we're filled up with shame. We come to believe that we can do something or say something, and be something that will make us all right. We even think we can confess our sins, then stick out our tongue and receive a Christ wafer and be ok again.

Whatever made us think that we could find something outside of ourselves that could save us and make us whole? We are already whole, and all that we need to know comes from deep inside. To keep life livable, we have to over-come our greatest sin; dishonesty with ourselves. We have to stay simple and honest. Most of the time we have to grow up in order to grow down. We have to un-do who we are. We have to un-see who we think ourselves to be. We have to un-be who we thought we really were. In essence, we have to un-do our un-doing. We have to over-ride those glaring, mean eyes in us who defy us to even dare believe ourselves worthy of asking and getting what we want. We must become the caretaker of our own childlike spirit, and never tell ourselves that our dreams are unlikely or totally outlandish. There is nothing more humiliating than to belittle a child's dreams. What a tragedy it is when she believes you! It's an even greater tragedy when the person belittling the child within is you yourself.

The very least we can hope for in this life is to figure out what to hope for. The very most we can do is to have the balls, come hell or high water, to live our lives inside that hope. When things are not clear, perhaps it's best to put them aside for a different day or a different season. We first have to find the *courage* and *desire* to know what we want. We then have to find the *courage to explore the depths of our souls* to find out who we really are and what we want. We might ask:

Is this the way I want to live my life? Is this the way I want to be treated or treat others? Is this the payoff for my efforts that satisfy me? Are my choices allowing me to adore my own spirit? What are the things I love to do? Who are the people I love to be with? What environment do I love to be in? What am I really good at? What do I do better than most? What do others compliment me for? What can I want that my heart is really, really into and wants?

When we discover what we really want, we *must muster the courage to say it.* We then have to find the courage *to mean what we say and live it.* In the living of it, we must find the *courage and compassion to weather the consequences.*

In order to grow we have to pursue places beyond the edges. We have to get outside our comfort zone and be willing to experience the unknown. We have **to ASK IN OUR OWN BEHALF**, and leave the details to the Provider Spirit of the Universe. As we say in sports, if a player ain't got the end game, she ain't got no game at all! "Don't ask. Don't tell" doesn't even work in the military! We must ask. We must tell. And we must do so consciously.

We've all made plenty of mistakes that could be seen. But it's the mistakes made on the inside, sometimes unconscious to even ourselves, that get us in deep doo doo. We must become **guardians of our inner thoughts. We must be honest with our inner** thoughts. We must edit our inner thoughts to reflect what we really, really want. Only we know to change these inner thoughts before they become words repeated and actions played out in life's dramas.

We all seek "the perfect partner" and yet we have a long list of those who didn't want nearly enough from us and those who wanted way too much. We all know people who have their hearts wrapped around people who will never love them back. So what exactly is our "evidence criteria" that will let us know that we got exactly what we wanted? Without clear criteria life is just one false start after another. In all things important, it is important to make a visible "purchase order list" of exactly what we want. At the end we can tell the Universe, "This or better!"

The secret to manifesting the change we seek, is focusing not on the **HOW**, but on the **WHAT** we want. This is the first step in allowing the Holy

Santa and all Her Helpers to release all their resources and conspire on our behalf. As soon as we ask with clarity and boldness, the elves of Heaven go to work to arrange circumstances, opportunities and people that are needed to fulfill our order. What we design in the inner chambers of our heart, will manifest in the outer palace of our lives. At this level, we must be honest with ourselves. Those who can be truly honest with themselves get far in life.

Garth Brooks got famous for his song, "Thank God For Unanswered Prayer". Ain't it the truth. There is a very fine line between being very specific about what we want, and leaving lots of room for the Universe to bring "this or better".

Intent is energy. Action is energy. If action violates intent, illness occurs. If you want water, you do not go to the top of the mountain. You act according to your intention. When you connect with your deepest passions, your life unfolds easily and effortlessly. By the grace of our good intentions we are steered unknowingly into our destinies. Where our eyes look, our bodies will follow. Energy flows where our attention goes. Ask each day, "What will I buy with my attention today?" We will never get anywhere if our thoughts are watching one thing and our eyes another. We must disciple ourselves to "be here now". We must be direct and ask. Nothing can be imagined that is not out there. Take your imagination seriously. Own your thoughts and act towards them with respect. What we seek is seeking us. Remember, INTENTION is a force that changes and reorders things.

Our thoughts are the building blocks of our universe and of our very lives. Our thoughts become words and words are arrows aimed at something. Our words push us into action and our actions create feelings that, in turn, attract the next event in our lives. Because we live in a resonant universe, our thoughts attract similar people and events. The world we see, then, is an accommodation to our beliefs, words, feelings and actions. This is especially true regarding ourselves. This world and our immediate environment came at our bidding. It is not an accident or unconnected series of events to which we are subject.

Here's a little seminar on magic. Step one: ASK! Step two: BELIEVE! Step three: CELEBRATE and give THANKS. Return to Step one. End of seminar. Remember, ASK BIG, because that's exactly what you'll get. Isaiah said, *"My words shall not return unto me void, but shall accomplish that where unto it is sent"*. Numerous studies show that the clearer and more specific we are, the greater the opportunity for outrageous success. We must be dead certain and delirious with Grace. We must ask, which thought or picture will I empower with emotion in order to generate a strong feeling? It is the feeling and believing that attracts our answer.

Bottom line, never live your life by the book unless it's a book you are writing yourself.

Chapter Two

BELIEVE!

A**B**CDE+L3+W2 (+/-X) = PMA

"Listen to me! You can pray for anything,
and if you believe, you have it; it's yours!"
Mark 11:24 THE BOOK

In truth, we are all like little children. When we hurt, we revert back to the wounds of our childhood. When we laugh, we become the giggling child of old. Wouldn't it be wonderful if we were still that big eyed, starry eyed, hopeful child, excited to be sitting on Santa's lap? There we could ask for exactly what we wanted and we BELIEVED that we would find our presents under the Christmas tree. As adults, we have the awesome task of becoming again like children and believing as we once did. Jesus said, "Let the little children alone and don't prevent them from coming to me. God's kingdom is made up of people like these children. The Kingdom of the Heavens belongs to those who are childlike". Matt. 19:14

Let us believe as we once did. We saw a box and transformed it into a clubhouse. We cut palmetto bushes and tunneled out towns and homes. We took Sears catalogs, cut out characters and clothes and made families. We built tree houses and made our baby dolls come alive in our arms. We were only beginning to understand the creative powers that live in us. We were a creating power. We were a believing power. We were an attractive force that brought parents and neighbors over to help us build our dreams. Just like children, we must know ourselves to be something very precious, something special. Let this knowing pull us to our true tallness so that we can re-discover the power of believing.

When we ask for health, believing, we ask for experiences in our lives that imply perfect health. We see through the healing process to the other side of having the kind of health that would allow us to ski, ride horses, travel to exotic lands, or witness the graduation of our grandchildren from college. It may be difficult to visualize "perfect health", but it is easy to visualize seeing distant lands or our children's children graduate from college. My love of the CBS Show, Survivor, pulled me into the vision of being on the island and playing to the end of the game. I totally believed that I would be selected out of the two-hundred and fifty thousand applicants. I ordered and wore my buffs all around town. I walked barefooted on my ranch to toughen my feet. I studied the game and the strategies of those who were able to stay in the game. I learned to start friction fires with bamboo and hair. And I learned to identify tropical plants and woods for food and fires. I started running, swimming, and working out at the gym. Long before I was in the game of Survivor Vanuatu, I was "in the game in my mind, heart and actions". Like a little child, I came believing!

Faith is believing that the universe is on our side. Children naturally believe that the whole world is on their side. Learning to believe again like a child is a very wise wager! You can bet your life on it, and often do without knowing it. The largest part of our capacity to do anything is belief. Belief is the bedrock, the foundation for success. To re-spirit our dreams, we must re-believe in our dreams. We must have faith in the very power of faith.

A believing is a strong conviction. It's based on our experiences. It is a tightly woven tapestry of thoughts so strong that they shape our lives into something brand new. A strong conviction is a deep feeling of already being there. It's an "already there-ness". We believe so strongly that we begin to act differently, and think differently, and even dress and behave differently. The amazing thing is that the entire universe shifts to match our believing. As Gregg Braden says, "We are never more than a belief away from our greatest love, deepest healing, and most profound miracles" (The Spontaneous Healing of Belief).

We ask for what we want and then we affirm that we are moving forward in the right direction and at the perfect time. We move fearless past our fears and comfort zones. We both envision and experience the dream fulfilled ahead and believe that we are already receiving it's blessings and rewards. Sometimes our faith seems small, so we command that we be emboldened to take each step with dignity, grace, and aplomb. We command that our desire to believe be strengthened with each step we take. We affirm that we are moving in the right direction at the right time with perfect guidance from the Universe.

When we resist believing, the very thing we fear comes galloping to our beckon call. Perhaps there is no greater teacher of the power of our thoughts and beliefs than to manifest the very thing we fear. When we keep company with doubt and fear we can only move directly forward to face the very thing we have created in our minds. It then becomes a matter of faith to step beyond our limited thinking, to see beyond our current situation and fears. Every day is just another day with all its sins and griefs to bear. Our past may be filled with doubt and fear, and countless mistakes. But our futures are spotless. We can begin again in each moment.

We are required to get very clear on the end results of our dreams. Then we must FEEL ourselves experiencing that result. Our feelings get our attention. They allow us to focus on our thoughts. Our feelings are the clearest indicators we have of what we truly believe. When we step back to witness our thoughts we become aware of our beliefs. We can edit our thoughts to reflect beliefs that touch our souls and move us toward our dreams.

Once we can feel the beauty of our dreams, we let it go and allow the Universe to bring our dream back to us filled out with details we could never imagine. We are not in charge of the details. Our limited vision and perspective can't possibly see the infinite possibilities available to us. The Universe is in charge of details. We are, however, in charge of **asking** for what we want and **believing** ourselves worthy of receiving the richest of blessings. **The one who can believe to the very end, wins.**

We might pray for the ability to "trust". God does not grant us "trust". God leads us into circumstances that require our unrequited trust. I was once told that my life lesson was to learn to "trust". My very life and happiness in this life now depend on my ability to "trust". I have my life to pay if I cannot muster the courage to TRUST! We pray to "believe". God does not grant us "believing". God orchestrates people and dreams worth believing in. One of the joys of "believing" at any place on this great web of life is that the impact of our believing is felt on another. We overcome our doubts and fears, not just for ourselves, but for countless others in similar situations to our own. When I chose life over death and "togetherness no matter what" over "divorce", I did it for myself and all the other people who are in similar situations.

Trusting takes lots of practice. It might take years to build up trust and only a second to destroy it. We must dare to believe and then stick to the row we're hoeing. Like sunflowers, we turn and bend to the light of our beliefs. We can only receive what we believe we will receive. I believed that I would live to write books, write and sing songs, play the game of Survivor, and I believe that the love of my life will be mine.

The changes we seek do not come with more holiness, hard work, prayer, kindness, or wisdom. The changes we seek come by being caretakers of our thoughts. Our thoughts elicit feelings, and our lives cannot explode into our dreams until we have all the feelings of excitement, thrill, hope, anticipation, confidence, passion, and strength. Hope reigns eternal. Change is not gradual. It happens instantaneously, suddenly, and is irreversible. You rotate into a new dimension with a change of thought. We must be guided by a single will. We must walk into life believing that we are a child of the King, deserving the very best. If we ask for one thing and prepare for another, we will get what we prepare for. When others say, "What if you fail?" I say, "What if I don't!" Favor the long shot in life. Finish strong! Faith is made up of a lot of MAKE BELIEVE!

The elders tell us this: "The answer to every question is in your heart. Open up your heart." We now know that the electrical signal from our heart (EKG) is up to 60 times as great as the electrical signal from the brain (EEG). The heart's magnetic field is as much as 5,000 times stronger than that of the brain. If our thoughts can marry our emotions to produce true heart feelings, we can speak directly into the creative flow of the universe. Our feelings, produced by the beliefs we generate, attract the very thing we desire. Our beliefs are expressed in the heart where feelings produce the electrical waves that mold the material world. Our beliefs and the feelings that they engender are the language of miracles and creation. Like the elders advise, OPEN UP YOUR HEART!

Let's pretend! How would you behave differently right now if what you have asked for is already true in this world? How would you think differently or feel differently? You would be filled with praise and appreciation. You would be in love with all of life. Pretend every day that you already have your dream. Remember, the Universe doesn't give a bugs fart about your degrees. It is only your degree of faith that calls forth magic. Faith and magic are the very same thing. Greet every day with a heart full of faith and walk on with Spirit as your guide. Expect a miracle! In fact, expect miracle upon miracle! Move only in the direction of your dreams. You must have staying power. **Ask and Believe**. One's ship comes in over a calm and non-resisting sea. Your ship is almost here. Stay the course! Practice having your dream every day!

My eyes already touch the sunny hill,
Going far ahead of the road I have begun.
So we are grasped by what we cannot grasp;

It has its inner light, even from a distance-
And changes us, even if we do not reach it,
Into something else, which, hardly sensing it,
we already are; a gesture waves us on, answering
our own wave but what we feel is the wind in our
faces.

Rainer Maria Rilke, Muzot, March 1924

Chapter Three

CELEBRATE!

ABCDE+L3+W2 (+/-X) = PMA

The Prodigal Son said, "I will go home to my father and say, 'Father, I have sinned against both heaven and you, and am no longer worthy of being called your son. Please take me on as a hired man.' So he returned home to his father. And while he was still a long distance away, his father saw him coming, and was filled with loving pity and ran and embraced him and kissed him. His son said to him, 'Father, I have sinned against heaven and you, and am not worthy of being called your son. But his father said to the slaves, 'Quick!' Bring the finest robe in the house and put it on him. And a jeweled ring for his finger and shoes! And kill the calf we have in the fattening pen. We must celebrate with a feast, for this son of mine was dead and has returned to life. He was lost and is found.' So the party began." Luke 15: 18-24

The only thing that stands between us and our dreams … are the thoughts we choose to think. Once we have gotten very clear about what we want, and have ASKED the Universe, the All-That-Is to accept this request, we must have the courage to BELIEVE that the gift is already given. This brings us to the next step. We must **CELEBRATE, IN ADVANCE** of the coming of the gift. We must **PRETEND AS IF** we already have the gift. This might look very different for each of us. Some of us sit in quiet, peaceful, recognition that the moment of receiving has come. Others will squeal like children. They will cover their mouth in great surprise and jump up and down. Some may experience winning a National Title in sports. Others may cry joyful tears of gratitude. What we all have to do is to SHOW the Universe what we want to FEEL. We must celebrate the feeling of winning within ourselves. When we are able to do this, the Universe will divine the circumstances, people and events, no matter how outrageous, that will allow us to feel wonderful feelings over and over again. Strong feelings are an attractive force to Spirit and will bring full support of the All-That-Is.

My personal response to being diagnosed with cancer and given two months to live was this: I went directly to Nashville to begin a recording career. While I was there I wrote and published a book. I bought a little cabin and wrote songs. I then returned to my ranch, bought four young colts and started training them. Oh yes, I mowed the grass! I produced concerts and training programs that allowed me to celebrate my life through music and ceremony. I lived and continue to live a life of joy and celebration. And, I continue to mow the grass.

Our FEELINGS are always attracting something. Feelings are the money we pay to have life at our finger tips. Earth is our school of EMOTIONS. We must FEEEEEEEEEEEL! Energy comes to an open heart expanding. When our heart is closed and small there is no energy. FEAR slams the heart door shut. BANG! No open heart equals no energy, no dreams, no joy! Perhaps the deepest hole from which to escape is a pit of real fear. Somehow we must find the courage to breath and move and talk ourselves out of despair.

Fear brings our lives to a screeching halt. It stops our thinking, our breathing, our blood flow, our digestion, our dreaming and our believing. Walking tall and believing brings a BIG HAPPY energy to our bodies and spirits, and then we are able to build the damn thing, whatever it is. We must say YES, YES, YES to life and find a way to celebrate the desires of our heart before we realize them on the physical plane. We must live and think like our prayers have come to pass. We must assume the FEELING of our desires fulfilled. Unless we enter into the images and feelings of desires fulfilled and think from this place, our dreams are incapable of being born.

We must give deep and genuine thanks IN ADVANCE for all that we have attracted into creation. We must use every breath to breathe life into our choices. We don't pray FOR something. We BECOME the object of our prayer. When we pray for perfect partnership, we become the most perfect partner. When we pray for a life lived in flip flops, we must walk through the snow in flip flops. We must acknowledge our choices and feel that our choices are accomplished. We must then give great thanks and celebration for our choices. The moment we ask believing, LET THE PARTY BEGIN!

We are all characters in a very large Dream. We must have reverence for our dreams. It is our reverence for our dreams that is the power that pulls a brand new life into us. Our dreams are connected to each other. Our celebration through dancing and singing and shouting and peaceful resolve feeds all our dreams. When we are able to come from despair and disbelieving to believing and celebrating in advance of having our dreams, we do it for everyone. We must gird ourselves with joy and gladness and awaken the fire and passion within. Without passion or the ability to light the fire within, our lives will dwindle away. Our fires will go out, and we will be very, very lost.

Barbara Kingsolver from the Poisonwood Bible says, "Sugar, life is no parade but you'll get down the street one way or another, so you'd just as well throw your shoulders back and pick up your pace". Fear brings things to a halt. It stops blood flow, heartbeat, breathing, thinking, and digestion. Feeling happy, with our shoulders throw back, brings energy to the body, spirit, and the making of all that we want. We are characters of a larger Dream. Our dancing and singing and celebrating feeds the dream. Without this, the landscape will flicker out and so will our dreams and our lives. Thus, we must gird ourselves with gladness and joy. If we don't have fire, we will get very, very lost in this life. It is we ourselves who LIGHT THE FIRE WITHIN!

We spend our whole lives building stuff and then the rest of our lives trying to keep it from coming unraveled. We must live and think like our prayers have come to pass. Assume the FEELING of our desire fulfilled and celebrate it. Unless we enter into the image and think from it, it is incapable of birth. We must give THANKS IN ADVANCE FOR WHAT WE HAVE ATTRACTED INTO CREATION.

Acknowledge the power of our inner technology and assume that our prayer has come to pass. Acknowledge what we have already chosen, feeling that it is accomplished, and give thanks for the opportunity to choose, and breathe life into our choice. What we feel deeply or image clearly will be carried out in minute detail. Mostly, we can image the best we can and allow the Universe to fulfill "this or better". We let this be our prayer and our believing, and our celebration.

Earth is truly a school of Feeeeeeeeelings! We must have the courage to FEEEEEEL our feelings all the way to the very bottom of our hearts. In this way, we will know ourselves and be able to be true to ourselves. The Heart is the center of Power. To open the heart is to find God. To find God is to truly find ourselves. The mind has no power without the heart. Emotions carry all feelings!! Our feelings are our pathway to God and Self. God is LOVE. LOVE is God! We are made in the very image of LOVE!

Invariably…Always…when big dreams come true…really BIG…there is a change in one's life…. Thoughts change, words change, decisions are made differently. Gratitude is given constantly. Priorities are re-arranged and optimism soars. THESE CHANGES ALWAYS, INVARIABLY, **COME BEFORE**, NOT AFTER THE DREAM'S MANIFESTATION!

Everything in creation is "over the moon" in love with us when we find ourselves. We must celebrate our successes before they manifest. We are in charge of our own blessings. The Universe does not make the choice of who to bless today. We do. The choice is ours to make. The Universe wants to be used! The only reason that some of our thoughts have not become the things of our dreams, is because other thoughts have become the things in our lives. We have only to look around to see the results of our thoughts. We are ALWAYS fueling something. We finance our lives with our thoughts. As the wise elders ask, "What will you buy with your attention today?"

Remember again, the single only thing that stands between us and our dreams is the thoughts we choose to think and the feelings those thoughts invoke. Think dreams into being. Celebrate in advance. Squeal, spin, dance, scream so the Universe, the Great All-That-Is, can choreograph all that is required to allow us to feel this over and over and over again. What's stopping you from celebrating right now. Get with it. Celebrate!

Chapter Four

DELEGATE!

ABCDE+ L3+W2 (=/-X) = PMA

"Arm yourself with vision, belief, and celebration. Then, delegate all responsibility for form to the Universe". Scout Cloud Lee

In the world of labels, I'm a serial ***driver*** personality. In fact, to be perfectly honest, I'm a driver's driver! In other words, I very much like being in complete charge of my life. When it comes to your own personal life, I'm a self-professing, serial, control freak! Yep, I admit that I'm deeply addicted to completion. Loose ends drive me crazy. Small talk makes me mad. I abhor wasting time, and I compulsively aggregate my energies specifically into purposes that I deem worthy of my investment. Sad to say, I once ended a delightful relationship with the sweetest man I've ever known because I considered myself to be an exclamation point (!) and him to be a dot, dot, dot (...). My loss for sure. However I'd rather stick my hand in a hot hornet's nest than hang out with people who are non-committal, ambivalent, and who don't complete tasks, and/or complete them well. The obvious result is that many times I've been heard saying, "I'd rather do it myself! By the time I teach you how to do it, I could have completed that task ten times. Besides, if I do it myself, it'll be done right!" Of course, right actually means my way. Yes, I am a pitiful disaster at delegating. And yet, I know that all things are possible when we learn to trust enough to delegate. Learning how to let go and delegate continues to provide me with lots of opportunities for growth.

In business and all areas of leadership, surrounding ourselves with extreme competence makes achieving our desires so much easier. When we figure out how to delegate tasks according to peoples' strengths and then stay out of their way, we allow them the space and freedom to succeed. My twin sister is an exceptional team player. When she looks me in the eye and says, "I've got this", I can walk away and never look back. She will perform, always beyond my wildest expectations, and always on time or early.

Because I can rely on her, I have the freedom to focus on the things that I do well.

It is a great system to work together with her. Things get done well and on time, which makes me very happy.

Mastering Delegation Requires Mastering Trust

Many years ago I had the incredible experience of meeting Adele Tinning (1906-1989), a renowned medium and "table tipper who lived in North Park, San Diego, California. Adele was special, well loved and respected by all who knew her. Because of her special powers NASA often used her as a consultant. Among the many people who visited Adele in her home were Elizabeth Kubler-Ross and Shirley Maclaine. To gather information, Adele would place her hands palm down over her kitchen table, which would lift and drop, tapping out words via the alphabet. I first saw Adele with a group of 50 people. We were so excited to meet her that my friend and I took a drum and gifted her with a drum song. We were crowed into her small home that was filled with bowls of candy and beautiful, fresh flowers. After sharing our song and before we left, Adele whispered to me, "Can you come back tomorrow?" "Absolutely" was my grateful reply.

Our two-hour visit with Adele was life altering. Adele never charged for her services. She insisted that we sit with her and listen to messages intended just for us. My message came from Jesus. "Jesus really loves you". I had grown up singing "Jesus loves me, this I know, for the Bible tells me so…" However, the skeptic in me couldn't help but question a direct contact with the man himself through an old-fashioned wooden kitchen table. That was quite a stretch for me. I even checked underneath the table for special wiring that could account for the table hopping up and down so often with such enthusiasm.

As it turned out, Adele said Jesus wanted me to know that my big life lesson revolved around trust! As a die-hard Scorpio, I'm not given to trust, unless it means that I trust people to be themselves, good, bad or indifferent. In the course of my reading, Adele told me that we would encounter some bad weather on our trip home that would detain us, but not for long. It was summertime and I couldn't imagine any type of weather that would detain us on our trip back to Oklahoma.

Also, before leaving, Adele told us that her stingy husband (at that time he had been dead for six years) had told her to give us each $50. We were traveling without much money and no credit cards. It ended up taking every cent of that $100 dollars she gave us to get home from San Diego. Her generosity was legendary and, for us, it could not have come at a better time. Our trip home seemed uneventful until we began to cross Queen's Canyon in Arizona.

It was a beautiful day. Ahead I could see a very dark strip formed "sky to earth" that continued to line up in front of us. As we approached the bridge at the top of Queen's Canyon, it suddenly became very dark and golf ball size hail dropped from the sky. We were forced to pull over and wait for the hailstorm to pass. The ground was totally covered with hail. The storm lasted no more than ten minutes. When the sky cleared we resumed our journey. Just on the other side of the bridge, the line of hail stopped abruptly. It seemed that the hailstorm had tracked us down and forced us to stop and stop abruptly. Our journey was delayed by weather, but only for a few minutes. I stopped doubting Adele's words, and then her message to me from Jesus came back strongly.

"Jesus loves you. Learn to trust in this lifetime." All the way back to Oklahoma my friend and I both strained to recover every word Adele had told us, mostly to no avail. I stuck with this wisdom: Learn to trust.

Over the years that wisdom has grown to mean so much more.

1. *Ask and you will receive.*
2. *Seek and you will find.*
3. *Believe and celebrate asking in advance of your dream coming true.*
4. *Trust then delegate.*

Those four nuggets of wisdom look deceivingly simple. Yet though I have practiced them over many years, I still need to remind myself to faithfully practice these skills. When it comes to delegation, I have to remind myself daily of my need to learn to trust.

Delegation Also Means Trusting God. This walk that I'm on has often brought me to my knees. During one such time, I pleaded with myself to stretch into trust. I was standing on our lanai in Kauai looking up the beautiful Wainiha River Valley. I had a vision that there were trillions of tiny little cupped hands reaching up out of every blade of grass, leaf, rock, palm tree, fruit, flower and structure. They were open to receive my dearest desires. The message from the vision was so clear to me. The entire universe was willing to take my prayers and dreams and hold them safely.

It was the first time I remember squarely placing my confidence in someone or something other than myself. It was one of those unforgettable, no turning back moments. I reached out from the depths of my soul and placed my heart's desire into "God's pocket" or "purse." there it stays, even today.

Logically, there are only a few choices of ways to manifest that are within my humble ability. However, when I am able to stretch into trust I can delegate my desires into the waiting hands of the universe, where infinite ways exist to manifest dreams.

My friend Carol Ann is a master of delegation. She, like Tom Sawyer, can attract a gang of people to paint a fence white and everyone will enjoy doing it. Carol Ann merrily dances from person to person bringing them drinks and encouraging them to work even harder. My own "I'd rather do it myself" attitude pales in the face of this model of delegation.

To be needed is a powerfully attractive force. The greatest gift we can give another person is to give them the opportunity to give their gift. As I personally learn to trust and delegate responsibilities to the Universe, I am giving God the greatest gift I can. When I trust other people I give them a holy gift and an opportunity to shine. As I learn to delegate my dreams into God's safe keeping, I am giving God the opportunity to give the greatest gift of all.

It is said that if a master really love you, they would set you free. We must be our own master. Ask, Believe, Celebrate, and then Delegate.

Whatever we want to find in life is seeking us. I'm learning that HOW my dreams are fulfilled is largely beyond my control. My question for you is what do you have an easy time trusting? Take a few minutes to ponder what you *can* trust. It doesn't matter what it is, just play with that thought…feeeel your way into it. Get all the juice you can from that experience and then repeat that feeling with something that stretches your trust muscles. From there, the more you repeat those feelings the easier and easier it will become for you to delegate.

Trust That It Is Done

When I delegate, my task is to simply trust that it is done, done well, and done on time. In a sense, I've programed my GPS and I'm free to relax and enjoy the scenery. Delegation sets the universe free to add in extra surprises for us and it's a system that works well.

Did I mention that I ride horses? As I write, I'm no spring chick but I still buck hay, stretch fences, put in gates, throw my saddle up, and climb on to a very frisky horse. I still tromp through snow and ice to feed my horses. I still feel my heart pounding as I ride and venture on to the trail ever aware of deer, dogs, armadillos, squirrels, snakes and birds.

Riding is a moving meditation for me and I find it to be a great way to practice trust. When I can completely trust my mount and myself, I can be swallowed up by each moment. I can simply delegate responsibility of the ride to my horse. That was an easy step for me, because trusting my horse is natural. Then, in this ever present NOW on the ride, oneness with nature is all there is for me to experience. Trust is inherent in these moments. Time slows down. I am more aware. I can smell my horse. I rock with the squeak in my saddle. I have seen beauty from the top of my horse that I could only see because I still have the courage to ride. I ask my horse, Makana, to take me where he pleases…he knows the way better than I.

This simple delegation to Makana was a small act of me learning to delegate to the Universe, and trusting the outcome to be far better than I could possibly conjure up. That was a breeze! When ancient Greek armies sailed the seas to do battle, they would burn their boats upon landing. They stranded themselves on purpose with no way to make it back home except by land. Making it back by land meant they must be victorious. They clearly *expected* to be successful and placed their faith in the Universe. The act of burning their boats was a powerful act of delegation.

Let's *Arm ourselves with vision, belief and celebration.* Then delegate all responsibility for the form of our dreams to the Universe.

Burn the boats I say! Burn the boats!

Shazam! The Formula

Ask and you shall receive.

Believe and act as if success were your only option. Celebrate pretending that your dream has already arrived.

Delegate then trust that everything has been perfectly taken care of.

Chapter Five

EASY DOES IT!

ABCDE+L1+L2+W2 (+/-XY) = PMA!

Our lives are intended to reflect the magnificence and wonder of a curious child entranced with continual imagination and awe. —Scout Cloud Lee

At Any one time, up to seven of the world's finest surfers live on the island of Kauai. They are often seen teaching the young kids how to surf. Their big lesson is this: "If you ever get caught in a big, bad wave, GO LIMP! Relax! Surrender! Give in! Shazam! Easy does it! Go with the flow! Flow with your go!"

Of all the elements of The Formula, Relax! Easy Does It! is by far the most personally challenging element for people to do. Me included. After asking, believing, celebrating and delegating, what remains is surrender. Tell someone to surrender and I guarantee you that they will come back fighting. Surrender is a button-pusher. In this instance it is not about admitting defeat. What I am getting at is that we've done all that we can do. Now it is time to relax and enjoy the ride in the very present moment. Our dreams are on the way. We've done our part. So, why not relax and have a little fun?   There is one and only one moment in time into which we can completely relax. If we are tense and distracted by our fears, we're locked in on what we don't want, and it messes everything up. By being attuned and relaxed in the present moment, from that peaceful place we are able to recognize and seize opportunity. That moment is NOW! NOW is all there is. And now, …NOW is all there is. Forever, …NOW!

In the Now Easy!

Relationships with horses have taught me the true value of living in the very present moment. Fritz Perls of the early days of psychotherapy became famous for one simple teaching: "Be Here Now!" Of course, as Richard Bach writes, "We teach what we most need to learn," so those teachings have clung to me and I've dragged them forward for almost 50 years. However, a good scare is a much better teacher than a thousand well planned lessons.

That happened when a dog fight broke out underneath me and my young paint colt, Dakota. He's a well-mannered four year old, with a teenage mind and experience. Having a hundred and twenty-five pound Akita and a new speckled cow dog get into a fight under his feet sent him jumpin' and twistin' like furry to get away from that commotion. It happened so quick that the only thing to do was stay in the saddle. A quick snatch at the saddle horn, a turn with the reins and a clamp with the knees is all that kept the commotion from putting me in the dirt on my butt. Thank God I wasn't daydreaming! When you're riding the trail, you gotta stay in the moment. You have to live in REAL TIME. In truth, it's the only actual time we have. Almighty power lies in the present moment. Even though our days might include writing a book or giving a speech or coaching a football team through a challenge course, or helping corporate executives create Leadership Agreements, we take the time to completely set our intention to live in the moment. It's a ritual performance that has probably added years to our lives.

Ridin' a trail in the woods is way different than running a horse around in an arena. A bunny runs across the trail. A deer and her fawn leap to safety. A bull snake slithers under a bush. The birds sing and time flies. Time flies when you're having fun. Horses teach us to love the moment. We love the moment so much that we think of little else. Taxes due. Grass needs mowing. Meetings, meetings, meetings. None of it matters when you're on a horse. We can focus on being our very best in the present moment with no distractions by doubts of the future or regrets from the past. In truth, nothing matters until the moment comes to actually deal with "whatever it is" anyway. When we live consciously and fully in the moment, we can gain the greatest awareness and control of our lives and our fate.

The best advice my grandpa ever gave was "Ride every stride, girl. You gotta be ready for anything and everything when you're on that horse." That has come to be great advice for life in general. Ride every stride! Live in the moment. Be ready for anything and everything. Relinquish attachment to the past and the future. Truly, by being purposefully present, we gain the greatest control of our lives. Training our horses for the trail has taught us the power of living in the moment and takin' it easy.

Here's the bottom line about the extreme power of "Easy Does It." *Our emotions are a reflection of our thoughts.* Emotions, not thoughts, are felt in our body. To know what our mind is thinking (and if it is thinking in the present moment), we must pay attention to our body. The feelings that our body is having are closer to the truth than a thought. Basically, our problems, pains and general cravings are products of the mind. As ole' Fritz Perls used to say, "Lose your mind and come to your senses." This is what trail riding forces us to do. We are forced to lose identity with our mind and become more fully present. The more present we are, the more joy we feel. We thus make it a daily ritual to climb up in the saddle and lay down the annoyances of our minds to simply take it easy for a while. The only place to be is "Now." It feels good to feel good. Training ourselves to live fully present is a great gift to the rest of our lives.

Lighten the Load

Make it easy! Take it easy! Lyrics by the Eagles (with a slight word change) remind us to lighten up and take it easy: "Runnin' down the road, tryin' to lighten my load...Take it easy. Take it easy." Take it easy simply means to relax and do nothing to niggle that thing for which we asked, believed, and celebrated having and delegated for the Universe to deliver. It doesn't mean to sit still or do nothing at all. Nope. We might, in fact, be very active. We are free to play, have fun, relax and enjoy, knowing that the Universe is actively manifesting our dreams. We can play while we wait for our dreams to arrive. We can get comfortable. Be at peace. We can now get centered in peacefulness; centered in a saddle with nothing to do but relax and enjoy. Taking it easy. Making it easy. Enjoying treasures of birds and trees. Our treasures do not glitter and shine. They instead nicker and neigh and snort and cavort while carrying us on broad shoulders that move with a simple sway. The asking, believing, celebrating and delegating are complete. Now the task is sweet surrender to the joy of this present moment as we live into the manifestations of our dreams.

All that we asked for believing is headed our way. Maybe today, might be tomorrow, but I know it's coming. When we celebrate, in a way we have prepared the baby's room, because there will be a birth in our home. The delivery and timing is delegated to the Universe so for now, we can relax, take it easy, knowing that we have already done a great job at attracting that for which we have given a great deal of attention.

I love the story of the old man who hired on to help a farmer with his crops. When he hired on, he told the farmer "I sleep when the wind blows." The old farmer was concerned about the statement, but hired the old man anyway. Help had been hard to find. Time passed and the spring storms came. During one very bad storm, the farmer feared for his crops and his livestock. As soon as he could he ran to inspect the damage he was expecting. Instead, he found the old man asleep in his cabin. Everything was boarded up and the livestock were safe in the barn. When the farmer praised the old man for his diligence, the old man reminded the farmer of his pledge: "I sleep when the wind blows." This was not a statement of fear or laziness. It meant that he prepared for the storm so well that he could "sleep when the wind blew." He could take it easy.

Taking it easy is an act of faith. We act according to our belief that our prayers have already been answered. Faith without action is dead, and so we prepare for our coming good. We receive what we expect to receive, and so we now relax and do things that make solid our believing. We now stand aside and allow the Universe to perform miracles in our behalf. We become miracle-minded. We wake up to leads and hunches in the present moment. We let God juggle all things in our behalf. Knowing that we are partnered with the Divine Designer of our highest good, we relax and play. Why not? We relax absolutely knowing that our good precedes us. We remember the great Law of Agreement:

> *Where two or more agree, it is done.*
> *Yep, it's that easy!*

Shazam! The Formula

Ask and you shall receive.

Believe and act as if success were your only option.

Celebrate pretending that your dream has already arrived.

Delegate then trust that everything has been perfectly taken care of.

Easy Does It. Surrender to the moment.

> *"Now may the Lord of peace give you*
> *peace at all times in all ways."*
> *2 Thessalonians 3:16*

Having ASKED, BELIEVED, CELEBRATED, DELEGATED, and TAKEN IT EASY, we must now **LIVE THE PEACE OF ANSWERED PRAYER.** We are absolutely the final authority of our life story. We are the author, publisher, and active character in our life book. It is our job to accept or reject everything that we hear, see, feel, and experience. It is we ourselves who give value to each thought. Every thought passes through our hearts, and only we can give those thoughts power to affect our lives. We must always aim at exactly what we want. We must never give power to a goal or desire that our heart's are not totally into. "Living" the answer to our desires, prior to our actually getting them is the way that we demonstrate to the Universe that we are committed. Asking, believing, and celebrating are ways that we demonstrate to ourselves that we are aiming toward something that our heart's are totally into. Perhaps the easiest way to LIVE our answer is to enter into the places of constantly COUNTING OUR BLESSINGS! It is the LIVING OF THE ATTITUDE OF GRATITUDE that draws our answer into our lives.

The proclamation, "You have cancer and may have two months to live" was an amazing blessing in disguise. My choice was life over death. I knew myself to be a beginning songwriter/singer and a writer. I decided to LIVE the truth of my conviction. I immediately moved to Nashville, bought a cabin in the woods and recorded my first CD. I continued to write music and began one of many books that

I would write. I strongly put my money, time and resources into "living my dream", believing that I would live. From that day to this, I begin each day with quiet time to reflect on my blessings and express deep gratitude for my life and my love.

The surface of the lake can be rocked by huge waves or simply rippled by a gentle breeze, but the quiet of a lake's depths is totally unaffected by storm or stillness. Deep in our soul is that stillness. This is the **believing place from which to live our lives**. This is the place of deep and abiding gratitude for our blessings. We must live life as though we are the last unconquered people alive. We must walk tall in the face of all doubt and fear and believe that our prayers are answered already.

Once we have clearly stated our desires to the Universe and experienced the depth of our belief that we are worthy to receive, and once we have celebrated our victory in advance, we must LIVE OUR LIFE COMPLETELY IN A STATE OF GRATITUDE AND "COUNTING OUR BLESSINGS"! We must hold hands together, but think our own thoughts. We must live our own unique perspective of life as we divine it to be. If we don't it will pass away unlived. No one else can live life for us.

We must grow a fixedness within ourselves, a true core around which we dare to live out the life of our dreams. This place is our **center**. This place is the place **of deep gratitude and knowing that our dreams are coming true.** If ever we drop away, even for a moment, we vow to keep a memory of this constant of gratitude that awaits our return, and return to it within each breath. The world around us is constantly giving us feedback on the thoughts that we hold in our minds. When fear appears in our heart, it is a call to return to our place of gratitude for answered prayer!

We must live as though if we lost everything we would still have ourselves. Oscar Wilde said, "My great mistake, the fault for which I can't forgive myself is that one day I ceased my obstinate pursuit of my own individuality". As we daily leave behind all that is not the purity of our soul's purpose, we will reach a place of simple vacancy. Into this place will flow our most abundant accomplishment.

It doesn't matter what house you pray in or whether you walk tall and bend your knees. It only matters that you **love your life**. What we feel deeply or image clearly will be carried out in minute detail. Through the works of our hands, our hearts will be known. **How we live is how we lead the way.** We must live so that we are never afraid for someone to walk through our heads and our hearts. We must journey to know what lies deeply hidden inside. We must never believe that another person's plan for our life is bigger or better than our own.

Like horses, we must live in the present moment. We must ride every stride of our life. We must love each moment. We must live each moment. We must drop the past and future. We must be the fulfillment of our heart's desire. We must become our dream living into itself. We must, in each moment, ride our own durn brand! We must pick a way of life that we can devote ourselves to and do it. We must do it through fear, and doubt and condemnation from others. Real courage is being scared to death and saddling up anyway. Sometimes it means having "more guts than sense". It means that when we must ride through hell, we stay in the saddle and keep coming, knowing that we have already reached our destination or desired state in our minds and hearts.

We must become our own best HERO. The best place to be a hero is in your own life. We must live with HONOR and risk everything to keep our honor. Others may offer us information that may allow us to act in ways that meets our needs and wants. This may increase our self-confidence. But only each one of us personally can leap into the total place of trust that says "I'm worth having my needs and wants met".

We all chase dreams down the path of our hopes. Sometimes we lose something along the way. We must learn that loving and leaving is a way of life. We walk through the valley of our lives, learning to love all that we will eventually lose to more life. We learn to let go easily in order for more of life to grow.

Never quit. As a small child learning to swim, I learned that "swimmers never quit and quitters never swim". With only utter exhaustion for company, I have worked and sweated, straight through fatigue that surpasses fatigue… and far, far beyond, to build the dreams of my heart. When I had no energy left to improve myself and my circumstances, I persisted to build something with hand tools and elements of the land. When I fought my way back from bankruptcy and had no money to build, I picked up a hatchet and built an amazing village. My village was later featured in the <u>Oklahoma Today Special Feature Magazine</u>. I've worked my hands and my heart by day and by night. And then I slept, only to awaken and begin again. To this very day, I awaken in love and work my skin into too much tan under the sun. There is no stopping a heart filled with passion and belief.

Like a child, I continue to live a life of believing in my dreams.

Love banishes all anger and guilt. Love picks up the shattered pieces and reassembles us. We are delivered through life by love. We are transformed by our own design of love and our courage to live it through hell and high water. When Japan was forbidden to make war machines, they made automobiles instead, and won the world.

It is time to avow love and peace from our very center and live it without pain and sacrifice. We have already given our lives over and over again. It is time to move on. In order to move on, sometimes we must have the courage to feel the pain of the past, and come beyond it. We don't know pain and hurting until we try to pretend it doesn't hurt. We must feel those feelings and be honest about them. We must cry our tears, but then give our "purchase orders" to God and live inside our believing.

In times of need, we must look around and listen for that one voice that stands nearby waiting to help us. It will be our own. We must never doubt ourselves. We must stop listening to all the voices in our head that taunt us and try to strip us of our power. Our true voice never taunts! It is welcoming. We must live to keep our spirit in readiness. Our own spirit is the most reliable ally we shall ever know. The trick is to stand and live center of our power, and still be humble. Go whole hog through this life and be willing to take the consequences. Live believing with a big E-Ha Yippee Ki Ya!

There will never be a time when it is not NOW. Now is the only time we need to choose our destiny. What is inside of us is all that we can and do give to ourselves and others. We must never, never, never, never conform at the expense of ourselves. The only reward for doing so is that everyone else may like you except yourself!

Stand center of life, now, in the present moment. Eat the food of this Earth and know that we are eating the dreams that lived in the hearts of our ancestors. We are drawing strength from their hands. We are nourished by their visions for a better life that they have seen in their eyes. We are embraced by their wisdom. Live in the present moment, with gratitude for all that has come before us, and know that some of these ancestors are me come back to eat of my own flesh and bones and walk into the destiny of my own dreams. Ride the river of NOW. Drop "driven" and try "drift"! Worship life. And know that true worship is the spirit of WONDER! Play the pretend game with

God. Pretend "as if" every single dream of your heart is already true in your life. LIVE it and LOVE it. Let all others live their lives in their own way.

Chapter Six

LET LIVE!

ABCDE+L_3+W_2 (+/-X) = PM

For most of my life, I believed my dad, Papa Ed, to be a peanut short of a Snicker when it came to caring about other people and their problems. A thousand times I've commented on someone else's business and a thousand times I've heard him reply, "Sister, it ain't none of my business!" He'd be happy now to know that "I get it!" Other people's business is truly NONE OF MY BUSINESS! For every moment that I've spent trying to "fix" someone or something, I've missed the amazing opportunity to grow my own dreams and experience my own wonder and bliss. "Letting other's live their life" and "minding my own business" has freed me from responsibility that was never mine. It has allowed me to take the deepest of in-breaths. It has empowered me to focus into the middle of my own dreams. A great weight has been lifted from my shoulders in the simple understanding of his counsel, "Let live!".

When I was diagnosed with cancer, the word spread like a wild fire. Letters, cards, books, home remedies, counselors phone numbers, and all manner of "intended support" arrived at my door step. At first the pile of cancer related stuff seemed harmless. But within a day I realized that the "stuff" reinforced the diagnosis and forced me to think about it constantly. With as much kindness as I could muster, I returned the "stuff" with a thank you note. I realized that my own life was truly no one else's business. It was my life to live and I had to divine my own way through the experience.

Rarely a day goes by that I don't catch myself wanting to offer advice to someone. This very day I watched a young father torment his small daughter as he tried to get her to walk down the beach in huge fins and then put her head under the water to snorkel. Fins are easily put on "in the water", and if one walks, they need to walk backward to avoid tripping. Additionally, snorkeling is a very adult skill and not intended for a four year old. The young father was clearly irritated that his baby girl could not figure out how to breathe through her mask and snorkel. It took everything in me to keep from giving him my "come to Jesus" speech about the appropriateness of his behavior! Obviously, if real abuse is happening to anyone, we have a social responsibility to help in all the ways that we can. "LET LIVE" applies to the everyday advice we give without even thinking.

Allowing others to live their lives allows me to stop judging people and start relating to them. I now know that what we think of others is what they think of us. What we think of ourselves is what we think of others. Every thought we think of another is a step is some direction. Our destination will be reached either through pain or peace according to our thoughts. We decide!

Our enemies are not relationships. Our enemies are old responses to relationships. One can never step on a new path without healing the resentment and bitterness of the past. Otherwise it will walk with us into our new situation and poison it. We must drop all judgments about others and let there be gentle and harmless caring between us. We can't try to change something over to our way without having it change us back. The only way to know the truth of any relationship is to be fully in our own experience of our own life. To this place will come what is good and right and perfect for each of us.

What an amazing difference we would experience if each person stood fully centered in their own experience and allowed all others to do the same. I have often imagined what would happen if we could blow the great Cosmic whistle that would send each person and being to its perfect, Divine spot. At first, I imagine great chaos and then a re-settling that would result in deep and abiding peace.

When we lack peace about another's behavior, we unconsciously push them to be different. If others are like me, they resist even harder. When you tell me I must, I probably won't, even if I want to. It is true that betrayals have bent me in one direction and guilt in another. My life has often been a balancing act. I have discovered that when I push too hard to keep something outside my thoughts, I fall into bed with the manifestation of those thoughts. Learning to release the need to determine results that involve others is the daily practice of "letting other's live their lives". People get along together when they stay out of each other's way. We must let the winds of heaven blow between us, and stay out of each other's way.

We come into this world stamped with half our father's genes and all of his history. The same is true of mother. Their mistakes and triumphs are part of our history. The only difficult requirement in life is to throw away all harsh thoughts of our history and re-write our own personal history fresh and new. We must thus, walk softly in this life, as though our life depends on it. We must respect what we don't see and understand. We must know that what we don't see, sees us clearly. Others are watching, seen and unseen. Always we are molding our own life by our actions. We must join with those whose eyes shine back to us our own self-respect. When we grow and learn, we gain something. But, we must also give up something. There are no free lunches on the road of life! We must give up trying to control or change others to fit our desires for them. There is a place provided in the tribe for every manner of person and disposition. By honoring all of life, we insure the survival of our species and the future of the only home we know. We also free ourselves to live our own lives to the fullest.

We cannot let those who do not support us distract us. Let them live their lives. Honor that which another chooses. We can't learn to trust another by reading a book. We can only read that kind of trust in their eyes. Chew words up for a long time before swallowing them or speaking them. It's easier to spit something out than throw it up. If we accept or speak words that don't fit us, it will cause bumps and bruises. "The Bible tells me so" just doesn't work anymore.

God doesn't need to punish us for our thoughts and actions. We are masters at punishing ourselves. The real test is not who wins the argument, but our refusal to let any opponent anger us. Once we know that no one can take from us what is already ours, we stop trying to protect it.

We must learn to allow Spirit to be the driver in all relationships. Without the spirit of love and respect, relationships are in real danger. When we play with God, we play with unconditional love and respect. As Gypsy Rose Lee once said, "God is Love! Get it in writing!" Real power lies in inspiring others to invest their energy wisely. We do so by modeling it ourselves. The more power over others a person tries to keep for themselves the more they are likely to fall from grace. We must give up all designs for power over another's life. "Other people's business is none of my business".

Papa Ed

Chapter Seven

LET GO! LET GROW!

ABCDE+L_3+W_2 (+/-X) = PM

As a child, I grew up with an enormous bamboo grove as my personal playground. I came to both respect and love this grass plant for its strength, utility as tools and building material, beauty, and superb play house and play ground. As an adult, I learned it's most profound lesson. Bamboo seeds are rare. Bamboo only flowers every 100 years or so. However, when a seed is planted, it takes a full five years for that seed to take root and push it's little head above ground. It is the most patient of gardeners who wait upon this plant. The reward of such patience is great. In the height of its spring growing season, the bamboo plant is known to grow up to four feet in 24 hours! No other plant seems to grow so fast or take so long to begin its growth.

Imagine the gardener who faithfully softens the ground and plants a tiny bamboo seed. Then, every day for five years, returns to this place and waters the ground, knowing that, in time, the bamboo will burst through the ground and race to the sky. It is probably easier to imagine the gardener who waits a while for the growth to occur, and then begins to uncover the tiny seed and inspect it. This, of course, results in the death of the seed.

The ability to plant a seed of desire or the dream of a lifetime and then, in perfect faith, allow it to grow, is the topic of this chapter. We worry. We worry some more. Then we remember the old adage, "Let Go. Let God", or "Let Go. Let Grow". We conjure an image of huge hands outreached, ready to receive the object of our worry or desire. We even imagine walking tall towards the outstretched hands and gently placing our desires and concerns into those hands. We might even imagine being able to turn and walk away, leaving our gift with The Giver of our breath. However, it is a rare and noble person who can avoid turning back to check in with God. It is a faith filled person who can leave their desires and their burdens in the safe keeping of the Universe and never look back. It is truly the peaceful person who absolutely knows that The Universe, God, The All That Is, The Great

Provider and Comforter will, in fact, bring about manifestations of Spirit that are beyond our wildest dreams. Such a person is who we all desire to become.

Every faith espouses some form of "Let Go. Let God". However, the deeper truth lies in the ability to "Let Go. Let Grow". We easily understand the importance of allowing a seed it's growing time. We also understand the importance of nurturing the seed with soft soil, sun, and water. The same is true of the seeds of our dreams. Once planted, we must allow them their natural growing time. We must nurture these seeds with the light of gratitude and believing. We must parent these dreams by living our lives in the state of having ALREADY RECEIVED THE FRUITS OF OUR DREAMS. In this way, we are truly ready to harvest the gift of Spirit's fruits. We become the soft ground into which these gifts can be easily given. We are the beneficent hands and hearts that gladly and wisely share these gifts. By LETTING GO AND LETTING OUR DREAMS GROW, while we live in the total faith that the fruits of our desire are already given, we mature into the perfect place to receive these gifts. As we risk letting go and letting grow, we become a part of a Divine and Holy result. It is a skill that we must practice daily and grow it until it becomes our unconscious response.

A Unity Affirmation tells us this:

When I have what seems to be an unsolvable problem, I give it to God for a solution. As I do, I imagine laying it on God's altar, giving thanks for the positive outcome that will happen, and then walking away. I know not to take the problem back by starting to worry about it again. I have let it go! I give thanks that, through God's guidance, all will be handled in the best possible way.

I can and do let go of concerns, large and small, because I trust God. One day at a time, I let God's plan unfold, and I feel at peace about what is happening. Certainly, I honor the commitments I have made, but I am open to a divine change of plans.

As I become more comfortable with letting go of trying to control my life, I discover how fulfilling it is to let God lead me. By letting go and letting God, I am part of a divine solution that is taking place.

Things can be true in 100 different ways at once. We must let the Universe handle the details. Leave the details to Mother Nature and the Universe. She will find a solution that is good for all of us. Just think of the end result and let the Universe work backward to fill in the details. Unless we are open to the possibility that what we want is not the only possibility, there is probably little possibility that we will get what we want. Accept what is happening. Heaven's perfect purpose is in charge!

Nothing worth having can be forced. Relax! The universe is in charge of details. We must learn to have faith in things that come to us differently and even better than we expect. The Universe is in charge of timing. Why be ruled by time? It's only a ticking hunk of metal! When we have done all we can, then we must do what we can't….wait! And we must wait, in faith, believing and celebrating our successes. We must live as though we have already stepped slap-dab into the middle of our dream.

Pain may come along the way. Sometimes we must hug our pain as if it is a lesson to study and memorize and never repeat again. Then we must let it go and grow into a vessel to receive joy. The belief system that has held us in pain and worry is not all that is available to us. Our egos will feel wounded, hurried, and worried. However, we must remember that EGO stands for **Edging God Out**! When we feel the push and pain and pull so familiar to our ego, we must

LET GO and LET GROW! It's an experiment worth undertaking with our very lives.

We have to keep reaching, searching, finding, losing, and finding again, letting go and letting grow... over and over again. We must do so because to settle for less is to sacrifice our very lives. We cannot fly until we reach our full potential. We cannot reach our full potential without placing all of it and ourselves into the safe, capable and loving hands of the Universe. It is only when we let loose ourselves will we truly find ourselves. We will never suffer a setback when we depend on God/Universe.

As I look out over the country side, I see tiny hands reaching out of every mountain, tree, plant, rock, bird, blade of grass, ripple of river, animal, and fruit. Superimposed in the beautiful sky are the huge, barely visible hands of the Universe. I see my intent, prayer, desire, or wish written on a tiny scroll held in the mouth of a dove. Hands reach out from the entire Universe to receive my wish from the dove. All the tiny hands blend into the great hands in the sky. I **feeeeeeeel** those loving hands receive my message and hold them close. I turn and walk away knowing that my prayers are tucked safely in God's pocket and are already being answered. Thus it is that I LET GO AND LET GROW.

Chapter Eight

WIN/WIN

$ABCDE+L3+W2 \, (+/\text{-}X) = PMA$

For almost half of my life, I have worked tirelessly for World Peace. The journey has brought me home to the truth of peace in my own heart, mind and life. Early on, someone told me that the manifestation of my own dreams would depend upon my ability to wish for something that would be good for the One and the Whole. I have come to understand that my dreams are more precious to The Universe when they include a benefit that will uplift as many others as possible. Always, in all ways, we must seek outcomes, results, and successes that allow for maximum value for everyone involved. **W2** equals a **Win/Win** result that adds value to as many people, places, beings, and events as possible.

Will and Jada Smith are often interviewed about their Hollywood relationship. Will is both mindful and consistent to say that his marriage to Jada is his "number one job". His job is not acting, or directing, or anything to do with making movies. His number one job is his relationship with Jada. He invests significant time every day to growing his relationship. He says, "It's not easy. We work at it. It's our job". In everything they do together, they seek a WIN/WIN solution. Everyone gets something of real value.

Bear Heart, a Road Man of the Creek Nation said, "There are two words people use a lot: Unity and harmony. You can tie a cat's tail and dog's tail together and drape them over a clothesline. You'll have unity but you won't have harmony. Harmony is a tolerance, a forgiving, a blending. It is subtle, soft, but very strong. In order to live in harmony, the common denominator that binds is 'loving one another' in its truest form." (The Wind Is My Mother, Bear Heart Williams)

HO'OPONOPONO is an ancient Hawaiian method of solving family and personal problems and misunderstandings. Ho'oponopono is based on the need for everyone in the *ohana* (family) to work together to aid in each other's health and well-being. Aloha is the spirit that ties the 'ohana together and it is the underlying compassion that sets the tone for ho'oponopono. Ho'oponopono is the purest meaning of Win/Win. Harmony is valued more than opinion. Maintain the flow. Don't hurt the harmony for any reason. Relationships are circles. Stay awake until all disagreements are resolved. Never leave frayed ends.

This was what Hawaiian Hooponopono Lomilomi massage therapist, Allen Alapai told me about his grandmother's teachings. "Until the day she died, she called herself Baby girl". Baby girl or baby boy lives in our heart. Our heart is the heart of a child. We do not live as children in our heart's alone. We have a roommate. The roommate of "baby girl or baby boy" is the Giver of our Breath, The Breath of Life, our Creator by all names. Our roommate is always present and gives us, always, unconditional love. God is LOVE, thus LOVE is God! We are made in the image of God. We are made in the image of LOVE. It is all in our hearts. Our job is to open our hearts. We are here to FEEL. Life is to be felt. This requires an OPEN HEART. When we are open-hearted we care about ourselves and others. We want everyone and everything to be ho'oponopono! We want balance and harmony.

We must work together as one body…hands and feet and heart on One body working for the good of the whole. When a group acts as one heart, they win. When respect increases sunrise to sundown, true affection is born. When two minds trade thoughts each mind grows stronger. In the end, each mind loses the identity it had in the beginning. Let us be little streams that come together to form the great river that runs to the sea. Let us be for the One and Whole.

Relationships are one long road of compromise, deep and wide. One priority seems to swallow another, but ultimately we can build a life together that means more to the world than either of us could have meant alone. Each thing held back in a relationship, builds part of a wall. Each little thing, no matter how small, adds to that wall. Then one day you discover that you are on one side and I on the other. The wall has become so high that there is no climbing over. We must start something new and share everything together. Working well with others in any relationship requires cooperation, teamwork, loyalty, understanding, tolerance, helping, unity, and amity. It calls for trust, caring, helping, enabling, empowering. It calls us to grow into unconditional love.

When we meet someone we dislike, we are seeing a reflection of ourselves…there is something we don't like about ourselves that we're not owning. When we see it in someone else, then we don't like that person, but in reality we are being displeased with ourselves. Remember that. People like to blame things they do not understand on things that they do understand. We get back what we put out. Period. Mean out. Mean back. Judgment out, judgment back. Love out, love back. Puck out. Puck back. Trust out. Trust back. We must become a light in this world to make other's paths easier. Light out. Light back.

In order to truly live with an attitude of Win/Win, we must truly know how to value ourselves. This is a surprisingly tall order in a world that begs for our attention and affections. We can only know our own hearts in solitude where there is no reflection from others. We can only truly know what we have experienced. We must never claim to know anything unless we have experienced it. Recently, a friend was amazed to discover how little time she spent alone. In fact, she believed that she was afraid to be alone. Only now, at age 56 is she discovering the joys of sitting, or walking, or running in the silence. A young woman at a silence retreat was amazed to discover that she could only sit still for a few minutes. However she observed an old monk who sat for hours and hours. Befuddled, she questioned the old monk about his ability to sit so still for so long and "do nothing". "Do nothing!" he remarked. "In the silence everything is happening".

From this place we can learn to gain perspective and personal power. From this place we can be true to ourselves about our own talents, beliefs, feelings and desires. From this place we can bring to the table our own truth of what would embrace a winning solution to all situations. Win/Win begins within.

Win/Win becomes important when two situations collide or intersect. Conflict is a signal to seek Win/Win. Always, in conflict, there is a point of common ground. It is identified by the issue that looks like conflict. At this place, there is something that both parties want. Discovering what this is can often lead to creative ways to satisfy both parties. Much of life intersects with others. Always, it is essential for us to be aware of what we want and what we are willing to do to get it.

Three times in a row my hair stylist failed to give me the "cut" that I wanted. I resorted to taking her pictures of my desired outcome. Still my hair was too long. I once again rescheduled to have her complete my cut. Our situation could have equaled conflict. However, I realized that we had common ground. She wanted to keep me as a client and I wanted to have her give me the cut I wanted. Rather than blame her for ignoring my request, I went back in and apologized for "failing to communicate effectively". She was glad that I accepted personal responsibility for my part of the mix up and cheerfully re-cut my hair exactly as I wanted it. I was willing to put my ego aside and step up to the plate. The result was wonderful rapport and a great haircut.

Win/Win requires that we learn to hold the reins on pride. Pride usually comes just before getting bucked off the horse. It's important that we weigh our thoughts carefully so that we don't trade them for trouble. When one has large thoughts on their mind, it is good to walk alone. We must let our minds and our hearts press together like hands folded in prayer. Win/Win is about being able to say, "My heart and your heart are one and the same. I care about what you want. We'll come together until our hearts share the same song". When people no longer walk the same path and when hearts are divided, the circle is broken. In these times we must come together again and seek Win/Win. The circle is sacred. We must always seek to restore its harmony.

Disappointment is an inside job. If we are unhappy with someone or something, we make it so in our minds. No words are more hallowed than kindness and the courage to step beyond our egos to restore the circle of harmony. We must turn old judgments into mere observations. We can have a silent talk with someone in our own mind and heart. Our talk will find them. We must heal the wound in our mind, in our emotions and in our spirits.

Healing is also an inside job. We must believe that healing is possible and enter into the belief long enough to FEEL healed and "at one with". We must begin the healing by closing the circle for ourselves first and walking forward with feelings of harmony. Subtle movements and thoughts heal from afar. Slow, gentle movements are close to Spirit. We must allow the feelings of harmony and reunion well up in our bodies. We are all members of the Human Race. We, in truth, are all on the same team. We are all here on a spiritual assignment to discover and assume our part in creation. Our beliefs make all things so. What we truly BELIEVE is possible, is. We must believe in Win/Win, feel it, and celebrate it, in advance of experiencing it. Every conflict is our unprecedented opportunity to practice the art of "creating harmony".

No matter how thin we slice it, there are always many sides to everything. Everything we believe to be true in one context can be absolutely wrong in another. We must learn to negotiate this world, not manipulate it. It's never about winning or losing. It's about rising or falling gracefully without bragging, boasting, whining or sniveling. Growth occurs when two people can bring forward a gift together. When we come together with another, there is the creation of a new spirit. It is the spirit of the new relationship. One person can only see so far down the road. Two people can see so much farther. A circle of people can see infinitely more. As Gregg Braden writes, we live in a Divine Matrix, morphogenetic fields, a holy blue print of life. A circle of people can align and change the forces of our planet. This becomes the mustard seed that moves the mountain.

To reach Win/Win and figure out the solution to a problem, we need to FEEL more. The heart must be totally involved in the solution. We must release the problem from the grips of our minds where it can only grow bigger or smaller. When there is trouble in a circle, the entire circle must grow into a higher place. A community is intended to help us grow through things. It is not there to make us feel small and insignificant. Win/Win relationships are at the heart of all creative endeavors. When we forget the importance of harmonious relationships, our creativity will dry up. The greatest achievements of our lives will have the blood of human relationships coursing through them. All results can proclaim, "WE did it"! Ubuntu! I am because we are! What really matters at the end of the day is that, despite our differences, we all show up to help and support each other when we really need it.

Chapter Nine

CHOICE!

ABCDE+L3+W2 (+/-X) = PM

Choice is our most sacred act. Life force does not direct or compel us. We direct it. Personal choice belongs to us alone. The power to choose is the power to change. Every second of every day, in every way, we are "choosing". Each choice we make builds upon the next. Our choices may be conscious or unconscious. No matter what, each act is a result of our choice. When we truly understand that we are the choreographers of our lives, we can fully take charge of our choices. When one is truly on her own path, she carries with her all of her pluses and minuses. Our intentions program us toward every outcome. Our bodies, like torpedoes, are servomechanisms that signal us when we are off the mark. Those gut responses or soft whispers alert us to "choose". We choose to either move away from (-) or toward (+) what is on the path of our intentions. Sometimes our choices can result in "mistakes". From these we cook wisdom and hopefully have something valuable to offer. Bottom line: If the rules are stupid, break them. If a place sucks, leave! If another person is a sniveling wimp, tell them to "hush, and stand somewhere else!" The choice is always ours. We must do what we love doing, be where we love being, passionately follow our bliss, and hang out with those who support and empower our passions and dreams.

Doing what we love doing every day is as important as paying bills, doing taxes, and brushing our teeth. We must chase down our passions and interests with focused curiosity. We must not let them get away from us. Others will compliment us on our strengths. We must pay attention to those compliments. They guide us. We must daily pursue whims. We must act on hunches. These are the ways that Spirit guides us. We must listen and respond with mind, heart, body, and soul.

When we don't listen we take wrong turns. Then we feel pain. I wish to hell we didn't have to experience things to grow wise. But we need the experience of making mistakes, of choosing away from our intentions and passions. I've made lots of mistakes.

I'm personally responsible for legions and legions of mistakes. If mistakes make us wise, just call me Einstein! Fall down, get up! Fall down, get up! Fall down, get up! Just never fall down without getting up!

Life is not "happily ever after". Life is what it is. It changes. Old things need to pass away to give birth to new experiences. The truth is, old things die hard. Our choices take us in circuitous paths, but always progress is being made. A plan is unfolding. We are growing and becoming something. It's a break through kind of day when we realize that we can intend to make choices to allow us to walk shoulder to shoulder with our intentions, passions, and dreams.

I've personally come a very long way since my mid-twenties when I achieved my Doctorate degree from the University of Georgia. In those days I was certain that I was the smartest person on the planet. Now I'm certain that I'm not even the smartest person in my house! In those days I tried carrying a brief case and acting smart. It stooped my shoulders and made me walk like a turtle with my head extended in front of my shoulders. The amazing thing is that I continued to make choices that moved me forward. No matter how many drugs we all tried, or how many doobies we smoked at Willy concerts, we still grew up to own our own homes, have respectable jobs, and pay taxes.

I wish I knew when I started trusting my gut feelings and my basic intuitions. In those days, my familiar voice was a very small voice in comparison to the legends of assuming dumb butts who wanted to assume responsibility for my life. Let's not forget about the dumb butt I was to want to tell others what was best for them! Somewhere along the way I discovered that I was human. I screw up. We all do. We must learn to fix our screw ups the best we can and then move on, making better choices in the future.

We must name and claim our mistakes. As we accept them for what they are, they will lose their hold on us. We will stop trying to cover them up. We will forgive our own blunders. We will forgive each of our mistakes and then do the work of bouncing back. That requires that we "choose" differently.

Relationships are not easy. In fact, it is probably a true template for failure if we strive to make them so. What makes sense is to grow relationships that are purposeful, respectful, honest, trustworthy and grounded. In this way we have a home to come back to when our road gets rocky. Most of my most important relationships are the other misfits I found on the road that had me jumping from one unpopular path to another. Always I have defined myself by being "ahead of my time" or "swimming upstream".

All the amazing misfits I've joined with have given me courage and strength. Many times the strength came from adversity, and each adversity has defined me. Somewhere along the way, I have learned to choose a path and stay on it. A wavering nature simply causes others to turn away. We must choose with conviction and stay on our path long enough to see if it has merit. I have changed and changed again by my choices. Some people I know simply win the award for "the least changed person on the planet".

Perhaps the hardest change I have made was my leap from the holy side of my spirituality. No one tried harder than me to pray, meditate, eat only vegetables, thank the gods for each bite of food, tithe and tithe some more, study the sacred texts, contain my feelings of everything except love, love, love, and always pontificate some wise message in the middle of every conversation. I even tried putting my face over the face of some Ba Ba Ra Ra and meditating to myself. Did I mention the wearing of sacred regalia out in public! My attempts to be holy brought me heartache. I totally bought into the victim/messiah role. Everyone has heartaches. We all bury our hearts at wounded knee. We all must dig up our heart, clean it up and out and hold it up to the light of understanding. Gratefully, paths in life tend to bend toward each other and we can step off of one path onto another. We do not have to stay on the path of pain forever.

The long road of healing our hearts is a road from deep pain and disappointment to freedom. Even though we have always been free, we must individually learn this lesson. We must learn that our choices are sacred and mold our lives. We must take responsibility for our past choices and our present situations. We must forgive ourselves our choices that brought us pain, and accept our current circumstances. Always we must ask, who am I today? What is now, in truth, near and dear to my heart?

We encounter CHOICE POINTS every day. These are windows of opportunity. We can leap paths and join a very different outcome. We can and must move our thoughts, our emotions, and the resulting feelings to a different new reality...a reality that is already waiting for us. It is possible to breath out one reality in a single breath, and breath in a very new reality in the next. The choice lies in between.

Gregg Braden talks about THE BUTTERFLY EFFECT. "Tiny changes in initial conditions can lead to big changes in a later outcome. To change an outcome of our future, we must change the expression of our lives in the present". A tiny change in a large system will bring about a vast change in the over-all system. We must make different choices; choices that move us toward our desired outcome or away from that which counters our desired outcome.

Every condition that we desire in our lives, already exists in the land of possibilities. It is our "choosing" that bends those waves of possibilities to bring these conditions into our present lives. Everything that we desire, already exists. It is our choices that call our "everything" home to us.

All around us mirror the consequences of our CHOICES. We are in direct relationship with the elements of our world. We must learn to carry no crosses that hump our backs or cause us pain. My maternal grandmother told us this: "You cannot always know what to do, but you will always know what NOT to do. Avoid those choices and your 'what to do' will come to you". My daddy underscored this teaching by telling me this: "Avoid those who compare you. Ignore those who ignore you. Turn from those who say 'it can't be done'". We all identify with certain beliefs and then we spend our lives defending them with our very existence. On some distant shore we realize that we are the ones who have chosen our beliefs (even those installed in us as children). We are the ones who choose, and we can let beliefs that no longer serve us drop away. Thus, we live (+/- X) in order to steer us into our future by choosing to live in the present as if all that we want is already ours... because it is.

Chapter Ten

YOUR POSITIVE MENTAL ATTITUDE: PMA!

ABCDE + L3 + W2 (+/- X) = PMA

It is the strength of our bodies, the wisdom of our heart's experience, and the purity and clarity of our intentions that determine the quality of our lives. Every day is a new beginning. No matter where we live, the sun rises anew. We begin fresh each day. There can be no better nourishment for our bodies and our spirit, than to awaken with a *POSITIVE MENTAL ATTITUDE.* Before we ever put our feet on the floor, we can direct our thoughts to positive expectations for the day. At the very least, we can begin our day with "a good cup of coffee and some PMA! At the very most, we can awaken with excitement for the opportunity to actually participate in the creation of our lives. We do so by embracing the simplicity and discipline of *THE*

FORMULA. To be awake and conscious of our ability to create our lives, we understand that we are the very source of **POWERFUL MANIFESTATIONS ACTIVATED!** In a very real sense, we become the "**Force**".

We **ask**, with clarity and specificity for exactly what we want. We enter into the **believing** place where we experience the **feeling** of already having our desired outcome manifested. We challenge any beliefs that block us from feeling as though we are living inside the desired outcome. We then **celebrate**, rejoice, and experience deep gratitude for the answer to our prayer in advance of actually having it. We become the celebrated **FEELINGS** of our prayers having been answered. We then **LIVE** our lives as if we already have all that we desire. We allow others to **LIVE THEIR LIVES** according to their desires. We mind our own business. We release all expectations surrounding the "how to's and when's" of our answered prayers. We **LET GO AND LET** our requests **GROW** according to the Holy and Divine mystery and magic of the UNIVERSE.

We live our lives with a **Win/Win** attitude for everyone and everything in our sphere of influence. Where our lives intersect with **CHOICES**, we continually **CHOOSE** to move toward all that matches our desires, and away from all that does not. In this way, we continually exude **POSITIVE MENTAL ATTITUDES** and constantly participate **in POWERFUL MANIFESTATIONS ACTIVATED.** We never ration our good thoughts about anyone or anything. We look for the blessing in every situation.

In each thing we do, we serve with love and joy. We understand that the good in our service has little to do with the nature of the service itself, but rather with the heart we bring to the service. We know that an unwilling heart soils an act by infecting it with feelings of resentment, anger, or mistrust. In all things, we choose to do or not do, and then only bring forth a willing and happy heart.

We know that when we think positively, others are more likely to do the same. When others expectations for us move to influence us, we realize that we may have attracted their expectations for a reason. We carefully consider our situation and choose to direct or redirect our focus in order to bring about new possibilities. We remember that attitude is always an INSIDE JOB, and we are totally in charge of our attitude. We know that anger and depression is a misuse of energy. As quickly as possible, we move to an attitude of gratitude, and re-activate our desired outcome. We either control our attitude, or it controls us.

By embracing PMA, we come to understand that we create our circumstances. We do so by conscious or unconscious design or we do so by our judgments and prejudices. That which we reject, stalks us. Should we attempt to seek revenge, we discover that revenge first runs away with us and then it turns around and runs directly over us. We learn to catch our feelings of judgments and revenge, then stand on our tiptoes to see past these feelings to the thing that would bring about a positive Win/Win for everyone and everything, Once we drop the scales of prejudice and judgment, there is simply no telling how far our hearts can open. Our lives become disciplined to positive manifestations. We become true warriors of love.

We learn that the happiness we create is fleeting. The universe is fluid and we are an active part of the flow. We can either "go with the flow", or we can "flow with our go". Always it is the feelings created by our situations that trigger our attention and ask us to participate in creation. Wisdom comes from our dance with creation.

The soil beneath our feet is rich with the bones of our ancestors. Always we walk on their bones. The energies of their life experience is always available to us to either incorporate or leave for others. Like our ancestors, we are small bits of time, nestled into flesh and bone. In between birth and death, we live out our destinies. In the living, we create an energy to leave for our ancestors yet unborn. Our positive manifestations become the gifts we leave our children and our children's children. More than brick and mortar, we leave an energy trail for them to follow.

As we live our lives from the place of **conscious manifestations**, we can begin to see the shape of how things will turn out. We come to absolutely know that we are co-creators with the universe. That which is hard in life will kill us or force us to look within. We become brave enough to experience our fears and our tears, and humble enough to ask for help. We learn that sorrow for our lives is a useless thing. We let it die and replace it with gratitude for lessons learned. All things die and change. The wind blows until it exhausts its strength. The fall grass dies. Trees live long lives and then topple. Within our dance with time, we create our lives. May we come to truly value the simple things, like a "good cup of coffee" and some PMA to start each day.

Our minds think thoughts. Our guts exude emotions. The marriage of thought and emotion creates feelings, and all of Creation allows us the consequences of our FEELINGS. Our thoughts drive the power in our emotions. Our feelings are the children of our thoughts and our emotions. **It is the birth of our feelings that divine our destiny**. When our elders say, lead with your heart, they mean, "What you FEEL in your heart is what you will manifest in your life. Open your heart. Know your feelings." Become dedicated to the shape of every plan that allows you to FEEL all the feelings that live with Love. To do otherwise is to live in bottomless foolishness. Let the object of each desire, each prayer, each wish be to achieve a wonderful feeling. As Gregg Braden says, "The object of each prayer is to achieve a feeling. That feeling that our prayers invoke in us, opens the door and illuminates our paths to the forces of the seen as well as the unseen." Ask, believe, and celebrate. The world around us mirrors the effects of our asking.

Let us raise our glasses to toast our successes loooooong before we experience them. Let us rejoice at the very thought of new found love so that the Universe can escort our lover to us. Let us dance the dance of our wedding so that the Holy and Divine Magic can join us together with our Twin Flame. Let us marvel at the ways of the Universe that entertain and mystify us. Let us relax in the absolute knowing that our prayers and wishes are the treasures of Heaven. Let us play with THE FORMULA like children in a club house!

THE FORMULA: ABCDE + L3+W2 (+/- X) = PMA

Have fun, Playmates! Have fun! Remember, when all seems lost,….it ain't! Get in the game!

Your Cosmic Teammate,
Scout Cloud Lee

If you like Will Rogers, you'll love Scout! When a director of the Smithsonian Institute met Scout on the set of STAR TREK: The New Generation, he exclaimed,... *"Young Lady, I would cast your image in bronze and stand it in the Smithsonian to represent 'The Spirit of the Pioneering Woman in America today!"*

Dr. Scout Cloud Lee is a master of "LIVING YOUR DREAMS". She is a breathtakingly, inspirational, motivational entertainer...a type of "Moti-Edu-Tainer". She is a speaker, author, story-teller par excellent, corporate executive and corporate trainer and Peak Performance Coach, song-writer, singer, musician, and artist...and she has a story to tell. Scout is a CHEERLEADER FOR THE 21st CENTURY who knows all about *"pulling herself up by the bootstraps"*. She has survived divorce, bankruptcy, artificial knee and shoulder replacements, terminal cancer, the loss of her partner, and 38 days on the CBS hit show, Survivor, where, at age 60, she finished in the final three. She has now become a <u>Master of Celebration</u> and a stunning feminine model of "LIVING YOUR DREAMS".

How we individually participate in the creation of our lives is at the core of Scout's work, play, and music. Scout walks her talk! She picked up a hammer and built her own Hogan style home, ranch house, cabins, and ceremonial village. She is internationally known for a communication technology known as *"THE EXCELLENCE PRINCIPLE"*, and corporate trainings called *"THE CHALLENGE OF EXCELLENCE"* and *"TRACKING PEAK PERFORMANCE"*.

Scout is the author of many published books, including THE EXCELLENCE PRINCIPLE, THE CHALLENGE OF EXCELLENCE, THE CIRCLE IS SACRED, SWORN TO FUN: Celebrate Every Little Thing, THE COST OF LOVE: A Compassionate Approach to Customer Service, TIPS AND TALES FROM THE TRAIL: Cowgirls Shoot Straight About Business and Life; SCOUT'S HONOR: Campfire Stories to Rekindle

Your Soul, and INTEGRITY AT THE TOP: Wit and Wisdom for the Workplace.

To my Readers: I'd love to hear your story. Please email me.

scout@scoutcloudlee.com
scoutcloudlee@me.com

www.scoutcloudlee.com
www.planetteamwork.com
www.drscoutcloudlee.com

Spirit's Time Has Come

By: Scout Cloud Lee, copyright, 2001. ASCAP

Sons and Daughters of the Stars. Tribal Members of the Great Central Sun. Sisters and Brothers of the Entire Inter-galactic Federation, Know this to be true!!! SPIRIT'S TIME HAS COME!!!

Giver of our Breath! Great, Great Spirit! We speak with gratitude for the LOVE that brings us into direct relationship with all things.

Walk on... with Spirit by our side. Walk on, with Spirit as our Guide. We hold ALL hearts within our hands. We trust ourselves and make a stand. When we dare, we know we can. Spirit's Time has Come!!

Our intentions are good and our devotion is deep for our children out seven generations! When we're off the mark, we know to step back on the path of our heart's desire. We command our feet to fit easily into the moccasins of all our relations that walk the Star Path Home.

We stand tall in the presence of all life's lessons. We hold back our tongue when our words would bring imbalance. We speak always to spin the sacred spiral that brings together all things in perfect harmony.

Keep strong the sweet aroma of our heart's-fire burning.

Great Spirit, we stand center in your Presence, which is far more precious than all of your many names. We command miracles here on Earth with the giving of our gifts. We see your wisdom etched in the lines of ancient elders praying power. We hear your love songs in the wind and see your smile in every flower. We feel your HAPPY in the waves of island palm trees dancing wild! And hold your love of simple things in the hands of every child!!

Walk on! Walk on! Spirit lives inside! Walk on! Walk on! SPIRIT is our Guide. We hold All hearts within our hands. We trust in LOVE and make a stand. When we dare we know we can. Spirit's TIME HAS COME! SPIRIT'S TIME HAS COME! SPIRIT'S TIME HAS COME.